Mary,
A Mother Waiting

RAISING THE MESSIAH

"Haunting and humorous, *Mary, A Mother Waiting* allows us to see the mother of Jesus in all her humanity. This beautifully written tribute to the girl who accepted the challenge of an angel and grew into the woman who could command God gives us a new perspective on Mary as she playfully enjoys life with her son, even as she anticipates the future she knows neither of them can escape."

—Cokie Roberts, news analyst for ABC and NPR and author of *We Are Our Mothers' Daughters*

"*Mary, A Mother Waiting* is not only a narrative poem that captures the unique relationship between Jesus and his mother, Mary, it uncovers the strength of the parental bond in all of us. It draws us imaginatively into the time, place, and culture in which Jesus and Mary lived, and in which the reader—wondrously—lives for a little while. The poem is a doorway into prayer. As a good poem often does, *Mary, A Mother Waiting* moves the reader into meditation and prayer. It is dynamic, full of surprises, and finally full of grace. Not only are Jesus and Mary revealed in a unique way, so are we, the readers."

—Dolores Leckey, author of *The Laity and Christian Education: Apostolicam Actuositatem, Gravissimum Educationis,* Rediscovering Vatican II series

"The poetic power of this imaginative account is in the very human portrayal of the journey of faith shared by Mary and Jesus as they both grow in knowledge and understanding of the Father's will. The key insight of *Mary, A Mother Waiting* is the provocative statement that 'We all wait until events answer the question.'"

—Aurelie Hagstrom, associate professor of theology, Providence College, and author of *The Emerging Laity*

Mary,
A Mother Waiting

RAISING THE MESSIAH

ARTHUR JONES

Paulist Press
New York/Mahwah, NJ

Cover design by Sharyn Banks
Book design by Lynn Else

Part-title illustrations by Ian Jones

Library of Congress Cataloging-in-Publication Data

Jones, Arthur, 1936–
    Mary, a mother waiting : raising the Messiah / Arthur Jones.
       p. cm.
    ISBN 978-0-8091-4696-3 (alk. paper)
    1. Mary, Blessed Virgin, Saint. 2. Jesus Christ. I. Title.
    BT605.3.J66 2011
    232.91—dc22
                                                                            2010040486

Published by Paulist Press
997 Macarthur Boulevard
Mahwah, New Jersey 07430

www.paulistpress.com

Printed and bound in the
United States of America

For the late Joan O'Brien,
my dear, devout, and determined sister-in-law,
mother of three sons and a daughter,
and for her husband, Michael O'Brien,
father of the brood,
and my great and good friend
of more than fifty years

There is little historical evidence for Jesus' "hidden years," the period from his boyhood up to the moment when he calls the first disciples. This narrative's true foundation, therefore, is in its dynamic spiritual interaction between a courageous, loving mother and a dedicated, visionary, and loving son.

Contents

Acknowledgments

The dozen or so people I asked to read the draft manuscript of *Mary, A Mother Waiting* contributed significantly to the quality of the final product. The shortcomings are all mine. It is a pleasure to thank Allen Coven and Susie Needle, Audrey Rogers, Alyssa O'Brien, Sr. Susan Wolf, SND, Cheryl Bubier, Cathy Bunting, Cokie Roberts, Ambassador Lindy Boggs, Rev. Richard Lawrence, Teresa Sanders, Peggy Shouse, Desmond Fisher, Gerry Fialkowski, Raymond Bahr, MD, and, as ever, Jean Blake. My apologies if I've omitted anyone.

Nancy de Flon, my editor at Paulist Press, provided the keen insights and professionally sharp judgment that give the work its luster. Thank you, Nancy.

The charcoal illustrations are by my peripatetic graphic-artist son, Ian, who completed the final one, the sandals, between returning to his home from Calgary and leaving shortly thereafter for Germany. Thanks, IJ.

My wife, Margie, kept to her ritual of never reading a word of anything I'm writing until it is published. Her decision is undoubtedly a key factor in our forty-eight years of good-natured marital harmony.

Introduction

I cannot tell you where poetry comes from. I can tell you where this book may have originated. In 1945, when Britain's husbands, fathers, uncles, and brothers began returning home to civilian life from World War II, I was living in Lancashire in the house of my maternal grandparents with my mother, an older brother, and a younger sister. I was nine.

We had lived through a lot in our own home during that war. The month I turned five, in May 1941, across a three-day period of almost nonstop bombing, 1,741 people were killed within a three-and-a-half-mile radius of my house. More than five hundred were buried in a common grave. My dad's brother the pilot was killed; his brother the tank commander would soon be dead. My father, exempt from military service, nonetheless left his hospital duties and volunteered. We moved to my maternal grandparents' home in Warrington, Lancashire.

Apart from the granddads, the men were gone. The women kept everything going. My mother, her four sisters, and the extended family of sisters-in-law somehow learned everything that was needed to keep us clothed when clothing was rationed and hard to find; shod when shoes were even harder to locate; fed when rationing and scarcity meant two ounces of "fat" (butter, margarine, or lard) per person per week, plus two eggs, two rashers of bacon, and on and on. It was an era when mothers-and-sons were the norm; fathers-and-sons were rarer than spotted tigers.

Then, in 1945 and 1946 the men came home. The women, immediately, instantaneously, were reduced to second-class citizenship as the men took over. They were relegated to menial duties, delegated their tasks as if the previous five years' experience had not altered them, too. It had, however. And it had also left its mark on a generation of sons who saw more clearly than most what courageous mothers did to encourage their sons to follow their dream or calling, no matter what. Even in wartime.

By 1940, before the bombing started, my father had built a steel Anderson shelter in the second kitchen of our towering Victorian redbrick home. The first bomb to hit the North of England hit our town, Birkenhead. And each night, as we knelt by our bunk beds in the Anderson shelter, we said:

> Our Lady of Mount Carmel,
> watch over us and pray for us
> this long night through,
> and keep us safe from all harm and danger.

We didn't know where Mount Carmel was, but we knew where we could find Our Lady: either in prayer or in St. Joseph's Church, which was directly across North Road from our house.

Somehow the mix of this past created the spark that ignited *Mary, A Mother Waiting*.

At the Gate

This is how Jesus came to be born. His mother Mary was betrothed to Joseph but before they came to live together she was found to be with child. Matthew 1:18

His longest time away. He'd said as much. It was
her not-knowing that hurt most. At night,
now there was no Joseph.

A dozen years back, that first trip, he'd blown in with
the dry *khamsin* wind. It sucked
tears from sad eyes.

Expected daily; half never-expecting him at all.
He came when he came: I met the
most *amazing* person.

Her mind jolted back, memories; scenes
of his first two returns crowded
her thoughts.

Back first from the Port, at sixteen, as day broke.
Fish on the dish,
ready to cook.

They'd embraced, cried. They ate. What has God,
Father, called me to do? Why do
I search this way?

Where does this lead me? Why me, Mother?
Mother, why *you*? Joseph emerged.
They'd embraced.

3

Returned from that trip, morning's arrival,
  eating fish; excited brothers, sisters,
  friends. Joseph beaming.

Father-son labored together. At night, James's
  house, blessed bread, eyes merry—
  stories they wanted.

He told them he had learned from listening,
  rarely questioning. An ancient
  couple's lesson when

A day north of the Port. So old yet hand-holding
  from love—and hunger. Too
  proud to beg.

He'd embraced them. They'd blessed him.
  That had surprised him, he said,
  and flattered him.

Coins in a purse. His last host had insisted.
  He accepted as a courtesy only.
  Dare he offer it?

Purse pressed into their hands, they knelt. No
  common tongue, he told fire-
  reflected kith and kin.

They kissed his hands. He'd knelt, kissed theirs.
  Tears washed scales from his eyes.
  I'll return with finer gifts.

The poor are going to feed in my pastures
  and beggars rest in safety. Ah! He is
  closer to the Father.

He looked away from rapt fire-glowed faces
to her. Mother, his eyes asked, will I
have gifts to give?

She reassured him, nodding, but hid her pain.
Not yet, she'd gestured. He'd
smiled. Understood.

Practical Joseph said later Jesus might have
kept coins for two Nazarenes. She'd
understood. Laughed.

That night, dark now, three holding hands
returning home. She and Joseph
absorbing his questions.

What was God asking of him? Joseph coughed,
embarrassed, unable to answer
or offer suggestions.

Jesus squeezed her silent hand: Asking of *you*?
She momentarily rested her head
on his shoulder.

She lifted it, said nothing, not knowing how,
or where, to begin. She said,
"Give me a few days."

He'd smiled. She sensed that and squeezed his
hand, and Joseph's, who said,
"Oh, you two!"

She'd replied, "Remember, we temple-retrieved
him. Twelve: questions, questions.
'Who is Abba to me?'

"At twelve he insisted he *must* know what this
meant. 'What do *you* know about
me?' he'd asked us."

"I remember," said Joseph. At twelve Jesus liked
to be at the well with her. Questions
with every bucket.

Her heart would race, she recalled, fearing to
acknowledge what she suspected
the Holy One intended.

"My rope puller." They walked on. He'd been
too young to realize she'd been
a child-woman.

She'd replied, An angel image told of God's
plan: a Son of God, Son of Woman,
Son of Man.

Son, she wondered, can we comprehend this
Holy One–gift? Holy One–blessing?
Holy One–burden?

Would she accept this difficult gift? She'd
welcomed him within her,
as himself

And as God's gift to herself and Joseph. Both
delighted. Alone: her joy
held sorrow.

She looked at him now, this man-son. "Did
you talk to the women during
all this traveling?"

Why, he asked, surprised, would he do that?
As if beneath his dignity.
She'd stiffened.

She almost responded harshly. Instead, easily,
she'd said, "Walk me to Ezekiel's
Grove, we'll sit."

They'd wandered slowly out of the village. The
path to Ezekiel's vineyard still had
flowers about to seed.

There, truly, his first long journey began. Rise
crested, they saw summer's end
laid out before them.

Olives gone, grapes long picked—though frantic
insects buzzed in search of
their lost fruit.

Joseph's clever bench circled the old mustard
tree's base. They would watch the sun
drop to blacken the day.

There'd be stars tonight if they stayed that
long, sufficient light for the way
home. They sat.

She reached out, held his hand, squeezed it,
said, "I hadn't needed to travel all
that way to Bethlehem.

"Joseph had. But he didn't want to be separated
from me at your birth. He knew I was
healthy and strong,

"But he didn't know pregnancy." She felt Jesus
    pull back slightly, as if he didn't
    want this particular story.

So? Sons this age uncomfortable with such
    accounts? So, his insights on women
    must come from her,

Otherwise, he might never have them at all.
    "About women," she said, "there's
    much to learn."

Speaking naturally, she found some words.
    "Without insight you cannot fully
    teach, reach.

"Therefore, this perspective: Women can be
    simultaneously strong and
    extremely vulnerable.

"Women ever-present, yet at the same time,
    invisible; in charge, organized, yet
    regarded as useless.

"Seen as chattels. What is a woman to think,"
    she'd asked, "when Jewish males
    protect, but dismiss?

"Males who give God thanks they were not
    born women? Honor women, yet
    see them inferior?"

She wanted to avoid annoyance, but she knew
    Jesus would hear, and would honor,
    her impassioned words.

"It's not only Rachel who cries for her
    children. All mothers cry for
    all mothers' children.

"They know so much more than men about
    lovelessness, neglect, loneliness."
    That startled him.

She'd apologized immediately lest she
    offended him. He assured her
    that wasn't the case.

He was listening, he said, deeply. She, as
    often, marveled at his desire
    to know. All.

She'd laughed, said even when she had
    questions, he always had more.
    He laughed, too.

He'd returned to his earlier questions. The
    Father spoke to you. Why
    me? Why you?

Does a woman forget her baby at the breast,
    or fail to cherish the son
    of her womb?

What does it mean? She'd taken his hands
    in hers. "For some things I have
    no answers.

"The Father had taken a step. God placed
    one foot on earth long enough
    to announce his Son."

Silence. Pouting? Perhaps not. Pondering.
    He reminded her she intended to
    talk about women.

Her laughter rang into now-starred night from
    the bench under the mustard tree
    in a chosen vineyard.

She told how she was a strong-minded girl,
    independent of character—
    and pregnant.

"Gossips said I had a secret." She laughed.
    "How little they knew!" Jesus burst
    into laughter, too.

He said the gossips must wait a while to
    learn of God's still-secret
    gift to all.

A duet of laughter. In darkness they'd
    soon leave Ezekiel's chill for
    warmth, home.

Joseph never traveled with a pregnant
    woman before, she'd told Jesus,
    in mirth, adding

Neither had she. She'd repeatedly delayed
    Joseph en route, frequently
    stopping to void.

She'd told Joseph she might deliver during
    the journey, and what to do if
    no one was near.

Joseph nodded doubtfully, she said. Jesus
   chortled that babies were not
   a carpentry skill.

Heavily pregnant. Riding and walking were
   equally uncomfortable.
   "I kept switching, so

"Bethlehem took two days longer to reach
   than Joseph intended. The
   rooms were gone.

"The innkeepers were surly, disinterested,
   bored: '*No one* has rooms.'
   Joseph panicked.

"He left me seated at that inn, to race madly
   from one place to another
   in the bitter chill.

"He kept explaining I was due. Finally, a
   kindly innkeeper offered his
   stable, at no charge.

"Joseph had been into the field to look. Cold,
   crestfallen, tearful, he'd come
   to collect me," she said.

"We were half-laughing, half-crying," she told
   Jesus, "but my overwhelming feelings
   were anticipation, joy."

She'd held Joseph, each consoling the other,
   him shivering as she'd said
   all would be well.

Wrapped tightly, they'd gone slowly to the
     stable, talking. Someone had
     cleared a low beam.

There was an oil lamp on it. Nearby, fresh
     straw, and two clean sheets. The
     stench: animal droppings.

The innkeeper had thoughtfully moved the
     animals to the stable's far end.
     The odor persisted.

Joseph brought in their belongings. He said
     he would remain awake to keep
     away the mice and rats.

She'd gone quickly into labor. He was born
     within twenty minutes, placed,
     wrapped, in her arms.

Joseph her midwife, her *hammyalledot*. She'd
     dozed and heard voices. She looked.
     "Two shepherd boys.

"They'd come in to escape the bitter wind.
     Surprised to see adults, astonished
     at a newborn baby.

"By lamplight, one said, you shone like a star.
     He brought shepherds' wives, mothers.
     Descended like angels.

"Ministering. Warm broth for us both. Two men
     arrived, told Joseph he could sleep,
     they'd watch for rats.

"We slept. Three of us. On straw in a stable,
   loved by strangers. My joy
   fulfilled, by you.

"The next morning the older shepherd boy
   brought his dog. There'd be no
   more rats, he said.

"Those wives and mothers lamented lack of
   space to share, but shared
   all else,

"Particularly my joy at their joy. 'A special child,'
   they said. Daily the young boy played
   his flute, 'for the babe.'

"Kindness, concern," she said. "Bitter weather
   warmed by generosity, by love
   for a baby. You."

The innkeeper's wife washed the sheets while
   she'd walked outside, to breathe
   deep cold freshness.

Joseph, finally, registered with the authorities.
   The sixth day they'd left;
   three of them.

Joyous farewells. Little gifts to carry. "Not a
   week old and already on
   your first journey."

Homeward bound from Ezekiel's Grove,
   she'd asked, Where had her
   words come from?

He took her hand. Happened to him at times,
    he said. Words just come.
    Even on a bench.

There was a night chill as they walked, saying
    nothing. Yet finding
    meaning in it all.

She reminded him of earlier times. When he, at
    twelve, wanted more, she'd said,
    Pray. Learn. Walk.

He'd walked. Again and again. Seated these
    many years in the darkening house,
    she'd laughed, wryly.

Walk? She smiled. She hadn't realized the
    implications of that remark. Was
    he just sixteen at the Port?

At twenty-one, his second return, no carpenter's
    bag held high. He'd given it away.
    Joseph's tools.

At twenty-one, his face reflected anxiety-etched
    gaiety, his questions spoke
    of harsher realities.

He said he'd moved closer toward an awareness
    unbearable were it
    not for Abba.

Yet a lightness, too. He oscillated, like a vine
    broken loose, wind-swung
    back and forth.

Swung between light and dark, fear and
   joy. Between flashes of knowing,
   storms of ignorance.

Swinging without quite knowing each
   extreme as his learning
   grew, he said.

After his second trip her learning increased
   as she conversed with this son,
   now a man. A rabbi.

His learning multiplied him, he said. Though
   living flesh, I sense, or know,
   I am timeless.

Frighteningly so. Abba is timeless. The son
   must be timeless. You who bore
   me, also timeless.

But Mother, how to accept, undertake this,
   he'd asked when returned from
   Caesarea Maritima.

Her answer was to hold him. In silence.
   Silent, he knew. Acceptance
   took time, love.

Now, awaiting his return from Samaal, she
   predicted he would arrive
   as night fell.

It was her game, played many times as day
   ended. This night? His
   head on her shoulder?

Where was he now? Had he reached Samaal
    a year and more ago? Not dead,
    not that. Unbearable.

Was he staying there? Would he send word?
    Where did the Father want him
    to end? Jerusalem?

She'd shuddered. The fright receded. He
    would return. She would embrace
    him, like after the Port.

His journey after Samaal would be finality:
    Son with Father. Did he already know?
    Again she shuddered.

Khamsin-whipped dust penetrated, irritated,
    as if there weren't irritation enough
    worrying, praying.

She sat in darkness. Oil long gone, lamp
    long guttered, she recalled
    his first return.

Glowing, she was, warmed by the sweet
    reminiscence of mother-
    son united.

The First Journey:
The Port

My son...do not reject your mother's teaching. Proverbs 1:8

Will Nazareth always welcome him home?
    Joseph had insisted he take
    his prized tools.

Joseph always said, the laborer is worthy
    of his hire. Jesus had liked that.
    Packed them. Gone.

To the Port. He wanted, he'd said, to hear a
    different wisdom from those
    who believed.

But from people who had never heard of
    the God of Israel. Of Jews.
    Who was their God?

He'd headed south. She knew that route,
    to Lazarus, Martha, and Mary's
    house. Bethany.

On to Qumran. Working, talking, walking,
    listening, always to listen.
    He had laughed.

You're always telling me to walk, he'd said.
    She'd squeezed his hand
    and laughed, too.

It's when you stop walking and start to
  talk there'll be trouble, she said.
  He consoled, she listened.

On, down the Dead Sea to Masada. Alas,
  everyone had heard of his God,
  knew Jewish people,

Even those with other gods. Onward. The Port.
  Aqaba. Such sights, Mother.
  Eyes delighted.

The Red Sea's headwaters. Boats in mad
  profusion, so jammed he'd stepped
  one to another.

Travelers, traders in Galilee are nothing like the Port
  and Aqaba. People flock to Galilee.
  Fishing, fresh springs.

But the Port? Tumultuous! Imagine! Take every
  person in Galilee, crowd them into
  Nazareth: The Port! Noisy!

What have you learned? Simple, he'd replied.
  An Arab will quarrel with anyone.
  If no one is there

An Arab will quarrel with the wind. Any passing
  Jew, seeing a quarrel, will join
  in and take sides.

She and Jesus had laughed until they ached.
  He'd seen the humanity of it all.
  Thank you, Father.

The Port? People never acknowledged one another
—push, shove, no courtesy, no ease.
Everything is money.

The Port! World's riches, spices! He produced
two little bags. Silk! A small square.
Soft as water.

Certainly, it is very exciting. Strip away surface
excitement—and? They have their
money. Their lives?

They talked hours into the night. Money is their
life. Money. How sad. How empty.
How understandable.

It gives them adventure, challenge, and, yes,
freedom. I'd mention the Father's
challenge, freedom.

They'd nod. They knew what they'd avoided.
The Port was Temple-teaching come
to life. As Baal.

This Mammon, the other ever-present God,
and anti-God. Not wicked men,
Mother. Obsessed, yes.

And foolish, yes, yet almsgivers, kind fathers,
honest husbands—many of
them. But blind.

Their emptiness complete when they
thought their lives most full.
How pitiable.

She'd said he could have seen the same
    here in Nazareth. No, it was
    too familiar.

These insights required distance, detachment,
    to make the texts sing to him.
    She pressed him:

She didn't want him forever gone. He replied
    he must see these things elsewhere
    in order to see at all.

Everywhere, including Nazareth. She knew.
    It hurt. Jerusalem's traders' wares
    are from the Port's boats!

He'd spent days at the water's edge. Repaired
    ships. Talked to sailors, taken meals
    with travelers. Listening.

All knew of Israel's Holy One, or Israel's
    people, even down the Arabian
    coast they said.

Then one day a dhow, grander than most,
    eased steadily to a wharf.
    It was anticipated.

Displayed: ivory, carvings, cloths the envy
    of all, he said, but his eyes
    were elsewhere.

The captain, dark as any Nubian, was not like
    any other. Jesus said he'd waited,
    watched, for two days.

The dark captain, his business completed,
    his wares gone, and soon to sail.
    So they talked.

The captain told of Samaal, of men inland,
    nomads who'd not heard of
    Israel's Holy One.

Sail with me, Captain Anzan invited. He'd
    declined with thanks, but
    promised: one day!

Then, back to Nazareth. Samaal could wait.
    That return meant a different story.
    From an innkeeper.

And now his favorite story, she told herself,
    seated in the dark, worrying
    and wondering.

His tale about a traveler to Jericho taken
    by robbers, left for dead near
    a crossroads.

Jesus would lean against the wall. He always
    began the same way: an inn door
    needed hinges fixed,

Existing screws pulled away from the wood.
    Jesus offered hinge repair for
    lodging, food.

Bargain struck, he began. The innkeeper stood
    there: could this man
    make the repairs?

Once that was obvious, Jesus would say, the
    innkeeper gave an account
    of the robbery.

"About half-mile from the inn, a man was beaten,
    robbed, and left in the
    road, bleeding."

The severely injured bloodied bundle of rags
    moaned, immobile. "Travelers saw,
    heard, kept going.

"A priest heard, crossed to the other side. Next,
    a Levite. 'It's no longer safe to
    travel,' they moaned.

"I know because they both stayed here. Told
    me. Late that same night, such
    bangs on the door.

"Maybe *he* wrecked the hinges? Hadn't thought
    of that—stick 'em on his bill. It
    was a Samaritan.

"Always ask to see a Samaritan's money first.
    Showed enough. 'A room,' he said.
    'Certainly,' I said.

"'For another man.' Gestured outside. A donkey.
    Man on it we got to a pallet. My
    Missus dressed the wounds.

"The Samaritan said he'd poured wine to clean
the wounds; honey for healing.
The wife approved.

"When the man was settled, the Samaritan took
food, ate, and gave money
for the man's care.

"He would return many days hence to pay any
costs. He did, said the innkeeper,
an honest traveler,

"A wonder. Usually take anything not nailed
down. Good work on that door!
More work out back."

In John's house, when Jesus told this story
he'd asked what it meant. Few
cared to say.

Some liked to hear it time and again. Others grew
tired of it. Some Nazarenes didn't
like Samaritans.

Weeks later, when Jesus returned with Joseph
from a building site, he'd told her,
God chose the road.

His Father had wanted him on Jericho's road,
not Samaal's. Not yet. What
could she say?

Shafts of icy anxiety penetrated her as spasms.
   Warned of worse to come.
   No explanations.

He'd be carried by winds blowing him onward,
   to what? Not wanting to know,
   she knew.

"How can your person contain all you are, and
   are becoming?" she asked.
   How can yours?

To Caesarea Maritima
—and Beyond

...enough for me to keep my soul tranquil and quiet as a child in its mother's arms. Psalms 131:2

He'd said tomorrow he must be gone. Yes, to
   taking Joseph's tools. After
   that? He smiled.

Came morning, dark village not yet aroused,
   they'd held each other, gladly, sadly.
   He was gone.

She had work to do; folk to help. She worked,
   wondered: Caesarea Maritima.
   Nothing but ships.

Her hand empty, she missed his. Traveling, she
   said. They always asked,
   fascinated, unsure.

Ships headed throughout the Mediterranean. Or
   across the world for all she knew.
   When would he be back?

In five years since the Port, he'd grown in a wisdom
   that astonished, tested, bested the
   synagogue's teachers.

In Jerusalem, too, they'd listened in awe. He'd
   worked to support her, just enough.
   He liked the hills.

There, he talked to God. Elsewhere he met with
  one and all. The authorities watched.
  He didn't mind.

They'd travel to Bethany to visit Lazarus and his
  sisters. En route he'd take his
  time in the Temple.

She learned so much, listening to his talk, his
  teaching. She told him how grateful
  she was for that.

She had not told him all she knew, or feared.
  Weeks, a month, two, then winter
  short, bitter-blowing.

This cold night, warmth stole into her hand. His.
  Silent embrace. He added wood.
  They sat, not speaking.

It was not necessary. Holding hands. Her eyes were
  closed, her heart open, warmed, in deep
  satisfaction. Praise God.

She offered food. He shook his head and smiled.
  Silence, warmth, each other—
  mother-and-son.

Each knowing what that meant. Later, much later,
  after they'd prayed, murmuring,
  to their cots.

She slept her deepest sleep since he'd left. Morn.
  He slept on. She'd sensed: tell no one.
  Quiet. Rest.

Fire lit as usual, water heating on it. Still he slept.
  Noon, no response. Gone two months
  only, but exhausted.

She stooped, half kneeling by the fire. Bending,
  a hand, then his head rested on
  her shoulder.

They stood, his arms around her. Her hand in his
  hair. Quiet tears, his ear
  warm on her jaw.

In tender embrace, loving trust; eyes, she knew,
  tight. Restoring each other. Her
  tenderness his.

Wondering, she waited. What had he done? What
  had he learned? Where had he been?
  Mid-afternoon now.

They ate, but he didn't go out. Finally: most
  amazing: Caesarea Maritima
  was sullen.

Bad weather held up trade; ships waited to be
  gone. Others, to dock. I met a
  young boy, hungry.

This Stephen, I shared my meal, looking for work.
  At thirteen, kicked out of
  a hungry house.

Told, too many mouths younger than yours. "Be
  gone!" Educated by a
  grandfather. Dead.

Mother, such questions. He asked more than I do.
  I talked of carpentry, a
  life of work.

They'd joined wharf-side casual laborers who waited
  for ships to unload. Ships couldn't dock
  'til others departed.

One ship's master wrote poorly, but large enough to
  be read from the wharf:
  "Carpenter wanted."

The knot of men was two-dozen strong. Other men,
  apparently not carpenters, were
  on the fringe

Of the throng, waiting for something to happen.
  Nothing else to occupy time.
  No new ships yet.

Stephen insisted they join the carpenters. Jesus
  demurred. Stephen shouldered
  the carpenter's bag.

The ship's master emerged from below decks. He was
  short, almost as broad as tall.
  He oozed strength.

He held a hammer, looked at the eager men,
  tossed the hammer high. It
  cartwheeled, spun

Handle over head, descending. The master deftly
  caught it. Challenged: "Hands up,
  carpenters can do that?"

The throng pressed forward, hands high. Each
    wanted the master to see him,
    and him alone.

Jesus had just watched, he said. The master looked
    at the few men who hadn't
    moved forward.

The man spoke to the two dozen. "I can find hammer
    tossers anywhere. I need
    men who'll work.

"Off to one side," he ordered the now-grumbling
    carpenters who saw the master had
    tricked them.

The master looked at the half-dozen remainders,
    "Any good lathe men?" Stephen
    pushed Jesus toward

The ship. Two others put up their hands. The master
    bellowed. A simple lathe came from
    below decks.

He planted the lathe on deck in view of all. This man
    enjoyed entertaining, shouted, "It's
    a two-month voyage."

One man walked away. "You two," he called to Jesus
    and the other man. "Up the gangplank."
    Stephen followed.

The weighty bag threatened to tip him into the harbor.
    The two carpenters then
    greeted the master.

Jesus said Stephen was his apprentice. The boy
    glowed. The master explained there
    was a test.

Each man would have two lengths of wood to turn
    into spindles. Blindfolded. The aim:
    near identical.

They nodded. The master pointed at Jesus. "You
    first." Jesus beckoned Stephen for
    Joseph's favorite chisel

And his whetstone. Jesus unwrapped the chisel,
    thumb-tested sharpness, spat on the
    whetstone, honed away.

Stephen, the stool. Hand on lathe there, steady it.
    Stephen nodded. Jesus fastened
    the first length.

Eyes covered by the master, Jesus tested the treadle,
    spun the wood a spin. Prayed, hands
    splayed on wood.

He had his measure. Gradually he built up treadle
    speed. It wobbled slightly. Hold
    it firm, Stephen.

He felt its new stability. Chisel raised, lightly
    applied while getting into a
    rhythm for turning.

Jesus soon had wood curls spiraling to the deck.
    Beige snow. The wood released
    carpenter's perfume.

Pleasant sap-smelled curlings flew. Chisel
eased along wood, spindling
inch-by-inch.

Jesus lifted the chisel, splayed his stubby fingers.
Tapped wood, resumed. More curls
drifted deckward,

Decorated his sandals, sat in the lap of his smock.
"That's enough," said the master.
Jesus stopped,

Lifted the blindfold, and looked at the spindle. He
laughed, Not perfect, but good for
a "blind man."

He removed the wood, handed the spindle to the
master, second piece in place,
nodded to Stephen,

Who handed him the whetstone. Jesus spat, honed.
The master again covered
Jesus' eyes.

Measuring done. A light tap on the treadle, a sharp
spin, chiseled perfume joined its kin,
'til the next was done.

Jesus handed it to the master, blindfold removed.
The master handed Jesus' spindles to
the other carpenter

Who shook his head, left, down the gangplank.
Jesus called, Good luck,
the crowd cheered—

Onlookers enjoying the show. Stephen beamed.
  The master looked at Jesus, "Does
  the boy turn spindles?"

Said Jesus, he will. Until then, I turn spindles
  fast enough for two. "Well said,"
  the master commented,

Slapped Jesus' shoulder, cuffed the boy's head
  gently, said, "Clean up the mess.
  We took on new wood.

"It's for the balustrades and banister supports you'll
  make. This Roman general a-building
  doesn't use stone.

"One night, two days, this wind, unless that wind
  turns to storm. Wood shifts.
  It's terrible ballast.

"You and the boy sleep below deck. We eat at
  nightfall. Sail up!" he
  called, hatchward.

Two crewmen appeared exuding urgency. Nodded
  to Jesus, gestured he follow.
  Coarse hawsers

Were handed to Jesus who joined in raising sail,
  stood aside as wind billowed
  the canvas.

Jesus rejoined Stephen. Get those two lengths
  of wood. Jesus opened his
  carpenter's bag.

Tools spread, Jesus once more explained each.
  Stephen handled them then
  sat at the lathe.

Jesus anchored the wood in the lathe. Carpenter's
  eye, he said. Showed Stephen.
  Stephen tried. Failed.

A dozen-fold attempts until, Carpenter's eye,
  Jesus nodded approval. Now the
  wood was level.

The ship sailed, two crew and master busied at
  their work. Focused, Stephen cast
  no eye to shore.

He was learning to start the lathe. Hand and
  treadle, together, said Jesus. Each
  time, the lathe stalled.

Each time it stalled, they laughed, for Stephen
  realized that with time he'd
  conquer it.

Night fell, lathe practice ceased. Time for food,
  talk. Vessel pitching. "Severe
  by morning."

Stephen, alarmed, asked, "Will we sink?" Jesus
  smiled, shook his head. Crew
  members laughed.

"Fear not! These seas, son, won't sink this old
  girl," the master assured him.
  She's sound.

"As a lad I sailed out beyond Aqabar. Great
   adventurer I was. Across
   to India yet.

"This boat couldn't make that, but here? Hey,
   she's too firm to creak." Jesus saw
   the master liked the lad.

Stephen, reassured, nodded to the master,
   who chortled, "We'll shelter
   afore the worst."

Jesus paused in his story-telling to look at his
   mother, concerned too about
   storms at sea.

Why worry, Mother? You know there's no way
   I shall die without purpose. Don't you?
   Her smile said,

If you say so. Jesus said, That discussion is for
   another time—not yet. Not
   yet, she repeated,

Mechanically, as she tried to contain her shudder:
   they'd acknowledged what had
   been left unsaid.

"You have so much to say," she said, changing
   the subject. "I've so much to learn.
   You'll stay a while?"

Years, was all he said. She sighed with relief and
   satisfaction. Not yet, then. Not
   yet, thank God.

She said, "The more I learn from you the more
   I may be able to answer
   your questions."

He continued his account. How next morning,
   ship pitching. Tied ropes around
   their waists.

He talked. She could not shake the chill in her
   stomach. Something had
   happened to her.

It was because both had acknowledged a future
   that was certain and could not
   be altered, denied.

She breathed deeply, asked God for help, and
   listened to Jesus afresh with
   a new appreciation,

A deeper realization regarding this honest man,
   her son. No, not realization,
   grateful acceptance.

This boy-now-man, whom she loved beyond
   words, who loved her,
   was hers to lose.

Carefully, questioning, they'd grown together
   in different ways. Sharing,
   living, praying.

"God, Father," she said, "I agreed, 'Do unto me
   according to your will.' Did that
   include my son?

"That you would tear him from me? Why this
way?" she'd said, back to
agonizing again.

"God, Father," she said, "let him, me, live for the
day and trust in you. For today, hope
for the morrow."

Jesus described how the master roared, "Vitesse,
go below decks now.
Young Stephen,

"Need to make the stacks fast. Cargo shifts."
Below-decks gloom. He pointed
to wood stacks.

"Stephen, lift one." The boy tried, and could not.
They weighed thrice, more,
his modest bulk.

The master nodded to Jesus. He, with effort,
shifted the wood, but did
not lift it.

"Stephen, now get one end. Jesus the other.
Lift boy!" They did, though
not easily.

"Lesson?" the master asked Stephen. The boy
thought. "Two can do what
one cannot?"

"No. Two can do more than twice what one can
do. Two oxen yoked together, boy?"
Stephen nodded.

"One ox can pull twenty men. Two oxen yoked
    together can pull fifty.
    Understand?

"They don't equal out the load, they make it light.
    Carpenters and ship's captains tend
    to work alone.

"But to lift they need help. Everyone needs help
    faced with large burdens."
    "I understand."

Jesus just listened. Then together they roped,
    restacked wood that
    wanted to shift.

This story made her tense. She had to ask her son,
    "Did the storm come?" Stood
    the boat on end.

The most amazing demonstration of skill. His
    enthusiasm delighted her.
    The tension eased.

The master was brilliant. No matter what the seas
    tried, he compensated.
    They stayed afloat.

More battering rains joined the winds. He
    obviously had a destination
    in mind.

He said an island was close. Other ships, storm
    shadows, headed in.
    He was first.

He let the wind drive him toward a cove at such
    speed the mind anticipated
    a tragic wreck.

But before the cove narrowed he swung the vessel
    around. Backward it seemed.
    Lines. His men ashore

Slipped, slid on vicious rocks. He played out lines.
    The ship was fast. They sat, buffeted,
    twenty hours.

Purifying the Waters

The child's mother said, "As Yahweh lives and as you yourself live, I will not leave you." 2 Kings 4:30

That day the master pointed, said, "Stephen,
    a freshwater spring, carry
    two skins, fill them.

"Take that path." Pointing. Driving rain. Stephen
    boldly jumped ashore. They threw
    two water skins.

A half hour passed. The saturated waif returned.
    "Dead animals around the pool.
    Men bemoaning."

The master asked the water's color. Greenish.
    "Copper! Spring's been poisoned.
    Last month's quakes."

Continued the master: "Quakes alter water
    courses in these coppered
    rock islands.

He swore. "Vessels rely on that spring."
    "The men said that." They looked
    at the boy. "Their water's run out."

Jesus said, Lead me. They leapt to wet land.
    Carcasses. Stench. Strange
    translucent green

Water coyly denied its poisonous nature. Sit there.
 Eyes closed. Tell no one. You
 do understand?

The boy nodded. There may be nothing to see.
 Silently Jesus asked, Abba,
 restore these waters.

Jesus closed his eyes. If it was to be done, he
 wanted only to see it completed.
 Not God at work.

A cracking sound. Jesus looked. Stephen's eyes
 opened. The pond was now
 overflowing as

Deathly waters seaward ebbed. The pond
 leveled. Another crack. The
 pond resealed.

Jesus knelt, took water in his hands, tasted.
 Pure, Stephen. The boy retrieved
 the two skins.

Stephen said, "The skeletons, dead animals are
 gone. Where?" Stephen,
 fill the skins.

Rain-relented day, they returned, skins full.
 The master eyed Jesus
 suspiciously.

"Who are you?" Jesus, silent, finally replied,
 The world waits 'til one man,
 then many, answer.

Next dawn they left on the tide. By nightfall
    docking, Roman general's wharf.
    Wood unloaded.

Five weeks as a spindle factor, Stephen
    was a novice carpenter.
    Jesus said, It's time.

The master knew. "Leave the boy. I have only
    daughters. He'll grow up with me.
    There's a vessel

"Caesarea-bound. Departs on evening tide. I'll
    take you to its master.
    Pay you off."

Keep half to raise the boy. "No, I'll raise him."
    Stephen wept. "I'm
    your apprentice."

Excellent, too, said Jesus. A good apprentice
    earns my father's tools.
    "These are mine?"

He asked in wonder. Frowned. "What happens
    to me?" he pleaded.
    He was crushed.

You have a new family. I have different work
    ahead. "Jesus, who are you?"
    Stephen asked.

Jesus embraced him. Stephen, later, you'll
    follow in my footsteps.
    Then you'll know.

Mary studied Jesus' wistful smile. Silent. That
    night he retold the tale
    in James's house.

Fire-lit faces of friends, family. Folks packed
    together. James, laughing:
    "How do *you* know?"

He knew Jesus understood the question. James's
    son asked, "Next time, may I come?"
    One day, perhaps.

James looked at Mary, then Jesus. "Leaving
    soon?" No, James, not for
    many years.

I must teach. To James's son: You will be a
    young man then. The boy asked,
    "Where will you go?"

To Samaal, to kingdoms south. To lands where
    people don't know our God.
    Or our stories.

"Where does all this lead?" asked James. Mary
    looked at Jesus. Back here,
    until the end begins.

More busy years passed. She, knowing without
    understanding. He, understanding
    without knowing.

Her heart ached, for she knew where it led.
    He taught, in synagogues,
    the Temple, and then—

He must leave again. I must tell you why,
    Mother. To rid my head of
    lies, the hypocrisy

Of these people who talk of God but do
    not know God, or they
    would be silent.

To empty myself, to refill myself, I must
    travel, walk with those
    unaware of God

To refill myself with my Father's words.
    I've known anger. These
    false teachers!

I must empty myself of those who weigh
    down people with laws that
    serve themselves,

Not God. They work in my Father's name.
    If I accept I am the Father's Son,
    I am God's voice.

She saw his distress and said, "Walk me to
    Ezekiel's Grove, for there
    we talk best."

An urgency made him talk as they walked.
    En route, they nodded to friends
    and neighbors,

But still Jesus was asking, questioning, am
    I truly the Father's voice to *boldly*
    proclaim? And then?

You know all the Isaiah verses we discuss.
   Suppose I just preach Isaiah
   at these hypocrites?

She knew—they spoke freely together—this
   was another prelude to seeking
   her guidance.

He often remarked that her commentary
   helped his thoughts. She was
   proud of that,

Yet she dreaded the cost, wracked as she
   urged him on toward
   dangerous tides.

Of course he was called. Any mother
   recognizes that in
   her child.

She couldn't not help. He needed this
   parental gift of "Go!" to
   fulfill himself.

"No Deuteronomy?" she'd asked. "No sweet
   or harsh psalms? What would they
   hear from you?"

He replied, Enough to want to oust me
   from the Temple, to drive me
   from Jerusalem.

Enough, she'd asked, to pursue him to
   Galilee, drive him from
   Israel itself?

Enough, he answered, to want me dead,
    when I tell them what Abba
    wishes I tell them.

Enough to say the Father knows: *These*
    people honor me only
    with lip service,

The worship they offer me is worthless;
    the doctrines they teach are
    human regulations.

My house will be a house of prayer for
    all *people.* Imagine, Mother,
    their response

If I added Jeremiah: *You have turned*
    my house into a robber's den.
    Imagine, again,

If I declared from Isaiah, *The spirit of the*
    Lord has been given to me!
    To me!

For he has anointed me, *has sent* me *to*
    bring the good news
    to the poor,

To proclaim liberty to captives, sight to
    the blind, to set the downtrodden
    free. They'd murder me.

How could they let me appear in public if I
    added, I was *the stone rejected*
    by the builders.

Can you see how I'd destroy their image?
   "I can," she'd said. "Yet you
   know the Father's will.

"In this, you alone carry your Father's call"
   —oh, God, her heart so hurt—
   "to face false teachers,

"To witness Isaiah's affront to them: *They*
   will hear and hear again
   but not understand.

"You taught me. Confront them, in due time,
   cast aside their rules with
   Deuteronomy, too:

"You must love the Lord your God with your
   whole heart, soul, strength, mind—
   and your neighbor as yourself."

Jesus laughed, Mother, it would be worth
   it just for the expression
   on their faces.

"But it will be worth it," she'd said, "whatever
   the cost. For this God has set you
   to fulfill."

Her heart was bleeding. "The time's not yet.
   Wander at will. Empty
   out the anger.

"Empty your mind of hypocrites. God will
   not let anything happen to you
   until God's time—

"I know that. *Then* the Father can fill you with
   his commands. This time,
   Go! Go in peace."

Mary looked at him, this man about to leave.
   This son responding to a call
   half understood.

He was almost twenty-eight now. Mature,
   learned beyond anything
   she understood.

They sat. Joseph's bench. He slid to the ground
   to rest his head in her lap.
   A living *pietà*.

It was never a wisdom key she possessed. He
   was wrong in that. It was her
   love abundant;

It was her heart-wrenched gift, so other-hued
   it pained. A gift of love only
   she could handle.

Jesus knew now what she represented: Love
   transmitted, three loves bonding
   to bind the earth—

Love from the Father to me, through my mother,
   coupled to her love for me
   and the Father.

She murmured something. Jesus looked up at her.
   "Son," she said, softly.
   "Go."

Tears flowed outside and inside. They held each
   other, waved as with distance they
   each grew smaller

On the steps taking him on that southern road.
   To Samaal? She sucked in
   her breath.

She was a mother still. She'd had questions
   and God had a duty to
   answer her who'd

Borne the Son. "My son, too!" she cried. God
   answered before the question
   was even asked:

She had her son. She had her gift. Earthly
   gifts were never meant
   to last forever.

The angel spoke in the silent way they do:
   Your son, God's son. You
   cannot understand.

She accepted, as she had the first time. She
   nodded, stared ahead at the
   now-empty road.

Yet, did she not have a right to be consulted?
   She'd served by giving
   Jesus life.

"It was not revealed at the time it would also
   bring him death," she told
   the angel.

Everything dies in its time, the angel said.
  You have him in earthly life,
  God has him

In him, with him, through him, in everlasting
  time. You and Jesus also will
  everlast together.

The Road Back
from Samaal

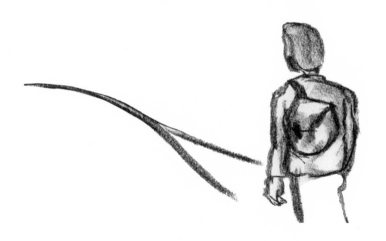

She was the mother of all those who live. Genesis 3:20

His worn sandals, barely holding together,
    slapped the path on, on,
        on to Nazareth.

Slapped against baked earth worn hard by
    feet, hooves, trotters, and paws
        long before.

Hastened on by the rhythm, drumbeat, cadence
    of three questions that lurked,
        behind his fear.

How to begin? How will I end? Will the
    Father be there? How
        to begin?

How will I end? Will the Father be there?
    Mile beyond mile. Relentless.
        Slap after slap.

His lips, eyes, his very being dry. The moisture-
    devouring *khamsin* burned
        the very skin.

Blessed dark. Night fell as always in an instant.
    Light then dark. Away then home.
        She was a shadow.

He tiptoed. She'd let the fire out. Returned
   to the house, his hand
   slipped into hers.

Did you worry? he asked. He'd never asked
   before. "Yes, as a mother. No,
   in God's name."

His head on her shoulder. She held him, ran
   her fingers through his
   grit-dry hair.

He keened. She wept. Sorrows ebbed with
   her tears. Joy in the vacuum
   of future woes.

She trembled, there would be no return like this.
   When Jesus met Mary this time—
   Oh, they knew.

No words. None even as they went in, he,
   slaking his thirst, went
   to his cot.

Next morning, he told her, leaving Samaal
   he'd reflected as waters rushed
   the dhow's prow.

Days on end, until he'd accepted: reflection
   provides avenues, only prayer
   provides answers.

Before that Arabian Gulf journey ended, he
   was talking to the Father in
   ways afresh.

Who will help me take the first step? Your
    mother. Is it true, Mother?
    He knew it was.

Mary smiled a soft, sad, answering smile that
    instead of saddening him
    brought joy.

Mary could tell from his expression that they
    each now knew what they knew.
    It would begin.

He knew how it would end; not time nor means.
    Father, will he be there?
    No reply.

She tried not to sigh. Compliance, acquiescence,
    those were not endorsement.
    Simply acceptance.

Acceptance did not signify embrace. No mother
    could embrace what was coming.
    He was here to ask.

Previously she'd never known when he was leaving.
    This time she would. This time
    she would send him.

In James's house, all eyes on him. Tell us. They
    had me stay. At first, I entertained,
    a novelty to them.

Darker people, kingdoms farthest south. Nomadic
    groups whose lives, flocks,
    follow rain.

Stranger walking with people, camels, goats, sheep.
    Not to teach, to listen. Learn.
    Welcome, stranger.

Not speaking their tongue. No one spoke mine.
    I learned. Worked. Shepherding.
    Words came.

Harsher lives than ours, Jesus told his friends. In
    drought, a nomad mother with
    newborn twins

Must choose which one lives, which dies. She
    hasn't milk enough
    for two.

In good times, newly delivered, alone a month in
    her hut, food passed in,
    waste out,

Again she decides. Can this child survive the life?
    Can it survive the rigor? Or,
    must it die?

They let their own perish, yet these people share,
    Jesus said. They share freely,
    from nothing.

The nomadic code insists: Asked for water, give
    half of all you have. Each
    still has half.

You travel, their impermanent tents yours. No
    distinction twixt family
    and stranger.

They offered me their chosen daughters, to wed,
  to remain because
  I understood.

Eyes in James's house eyes brightened. Jesus wed?
  I said I was already wed,
  to the world.

Though they did not understand, they accepted
  without question, as they
  had accepted me.

We Galileans, a friendly but tighter people, Jesus
  said, sharing, hold back nothing
  except, perhaps, spirit.

In James's house: Tell of us warriors. He did, of
  tyrants, sultans, desert chieftains,
  sleek dhows.

His eyes glowed. These lands attract me, he said,
  but there's no longer time.
  Why not?

Jesus replied, a boy knew his greatest attribute
  was he loved people. He
  would *meet* them.

Meet the entire world. As a man he saw it could
  not be, so he would not *meet*
  it, but *tell* it.

He would tell the world of his love. One day, on
  desert fringes he'd stood alone,
  praying, pondering

When suddenly the Father sent him home. Was I,
    or the Holy One, talking
    to my heart?

Jesus asked. Did that mean now was the time to
    tell the world? His friends
    did not answer.

Answer-less, some understood. Next day
    mother and son visited many
    neighbors.

Doubting folk who weren't interested; thought
    Jesus a wanderer who'd
    never settled,

Should have followed his father's carpentry.
    Just an idle talker,
    they said.

Others sought answers in his face. Feelings
    they couldn't explain: Jesus,
    strange *and* normal,

Earthly *and* holy. Holy One–touched. There, they
    had said it. "Our" Jesus.
    Holy One–touched

Who exudes wisdom beyond years spent among
    the wise. Holy One–touched.
    They said it again.

Jesus knew they'd said it, fought back tears of joy,
    fought fright's shivers,
    unworthiness.

Everywhere he told his tales. They pressed for
   the poisoned pool, nomad mothers.
   Their questions!

Tender listening, she saw—though disturbed by
   his challenges—they loved him, his
   humor, questions.

Are you going away? Half hoping "no" for his
   company; "yes" for
   more stories.

Not for months, he said. Then I shall leave to teach;
   a return unlike any other.
   Mary knew.

Once in James's home her eyes had said—she
   had a final gift to give.
   Hers alone.

Ezekiel's Grove Benediction

The mother was the last to die, after her sons. 2 Maccabees 7:42

Now, beneath this mustard tree in Ezekiel's Grove,
   as he asks, she knows, she
   must answer.

Grief inhibits breath. For the only time in her life she
   spoke without speaking. He heard
   without hearing.

The only way, for words aloud could not convey
   what wordlessness
   transmits.

She spoke of the angel-voice, an angel image of
   the Holy One's voice,
   not to be heard

Directly, as the Holy One's face was not to be
   seen. Jesus, eyes closed,
   saw his mother's

Silent warming words forming, but he shook
   his head. Not yet, he
   said. Not yet.

She was silent. He said, First they must visit all
   their friends, journeying
   only together.

In the synagogue they asked him to teach. He
　　begged off, asked for
　　their indulgence.

This day they drifted away to let him pray. Then
　　back on the road.
　　To Bethany,

To Lazarus, Martha, and Mary. Midday, resting in
　　shade as the donkeys
　　grazed, brayed.

Jesus looked up. His head was in his mother's
　　lap as she leaned against
　　the tree trunk.

From her. This day on Bethany's road.
　　the answer must, will.
　　come from her.

Did Holy One's angel tell you who I am? What
　　is to happen? And who
　　is my father?

My *Father*? *Abba*? What does it mean? Jesus
　　closed his eyes to shield his
　　troubled soul.

She smiled at sons unaware mothers see all,
　　acknowledge no masks,
　　as she said,

"The angel assured us both that the Father's
　　love and your mother's
　　are one.

"Accept this: my love for you is the Father's
    love through me
    for you.

"The Father's love is the love of both mother and
    Father. *You* are *all* sons
    and daughters."

Just as you are all mothers, he said, and Father all
    fathers. She replied, "You
    knew, then,

But didn't understand." He stood, said, always.
    He helped her up. A young
    woman still,

Sixteen years only beyond him. They embraced,
    smiling, laughing. Onward.
    To Bethany.

Lazarus, come out! We're here. Martha! Mary!
    Meet your mother. "Master,"
    Mary called him

As she ran into his arms. Shsssh! Not Master
    yet. Jesus realized this
    Mary understood,

Had awakened to who he was, perhaps before
    he had himself. Now
    here's Martha.

She, slightly restrained, kissed him. Not Lazarus,
    arms flung wide, firm around
    Jesus' back,

Kissed his cheeks. These were friends. Other selves
   whose love was constant.
   Absences forgiven,

Presence rejoiced. Later Lazarus on the other pallet,
   sleep-defying 'til "cock crow,"
   ever talking.

She knew he was happy at a time when contentment
   would vanish and never be
   his in this life.

She and Martha looked to the day and headed to the
   market. He, Lazarus, and
   Mary talked.

Loving, kindly Lazarus, never questioning yet
   reassuring. Mary probed, knew,
   like his mother.

From Bethany as they returned to Nazareth:
   He recounted how, alone,
   in strange places

He'd lain, seeing great things to do in God's
   name; then he would
   shudder, afraid.

Touched by God he could confront the world,
   he said, but not
   without God.

Witness he can, to a world that does not want, yet
   needs, to be confronted by
   God's demands

For love, for true repentance, reordering life to
serve God through
serving others.

For the rest, nothing in the world seems substantial
to him, he said, except
the Spirit's gifts.

Sometimes his mind wasn't big enough to hold it.
Pondering, reflecting was
so unsettling.

He felt, he said, a power around him, within him,
that frightened him. Could
he control it?

Will it control me? She listened and looked as
he struggled. He was not
so much

Speaking to her, as to himself. He burned from
the searing power of
God's love,

But was afraid that the Father would not be
there, actually with
him when he

Needed Abba, at that moment when he must
relinquish the power
and let go.

Without God he was lost, he said. Mother, help me.
She turned to him on that road
back to Nazareth,

"All is well, and all will be well, even in death.
     We all die, we all fear death.
     You are human.

"Fear death and accept your fear. As I fear mine,
     fear yours with love's
     overpowering trust.

"Does our love for each other die because we're
     dead?" He thought, shook
     his head. She

Told him, "When no one is left who remembers
     my love, my love lives.
     Love *is!*

"Which means love *always* is. Your love can never
     die." A pause. "*Where* did my
     words come from?"

Jesus said scribes and Pharisees were finding him
     provocative; talked of his knowing
     revolutionaries.

He talked to everyone. Neighbors were saying,
     "Don't let him anger
     the Romans."

She said one neighbor warned, "A word to the
     wise." I told him, "Wisdom
     requires action."

She knew Jesus sought no special privileges
     from the Father;
     nor did she.

They were there to trust in God. Her role: to
    love her son. They
    reached home.

Jesus, she knew, was eager to start the work
    ahead. He waited, a pacing
    caged bear

As she counseled, not yet, not yet. Then it was
    spring. "Walk me to
    Ezekiel's Grove."

It was nearing his time. Birds, buds, the promise of
    bounty—in opening leaves and
    greening fields.

They walked, talked about family, friends. She
    said she knew for certain
    he was God's.

Still he asked her, When do I begin? They neared
    the grove. She replied, "Very
    soon. Patience."

His visit with the baptizer had encouraged him.
    Jesus had gathered men around
    him whom she liked.

She'd laughed when he told her he'd told the
    fishermen, "I will make you
    fishers of men."

On Joseph's bench she said, "This was my school.
    You've taught me." You've taught
    me love, he replied.

She had to ask. "What am I to do after your death?"
  Be yourself, he said. She responded,
  "Who do you say I am?"

They smiled at one another. My mother. "They will
  come to me for cures, for protection."
  Do, say, nothing.

"The authorities will accuse me as they accuse you."
  No, you are only a woman. They
  both winced.

She was not offended for herself, but anxious
  for Jesus. Romans would
  not harm her.

"Yet the people will not know I cannot help them.
  They'll come to me. I have
  nothing for them."

It's how he felt much of the time, he said. My gift
  to them comes later; yours
  is now, in me.

Be with me in my ministry. Stay close to me. I
  need you there. *Everyone* needs
  you as mother.

You are strength when ours fails. She nodded.
  "What would you have people
  know?" she asked.

That I died a failure in the eyes of all except God,
  and you, and those who
  could believe.

"I am glad Joseph is dead. He could not have lived
    through this," she said; reached to
    hold his hand.

"Two days from now your cousin is being married.
    You must come with me
    then, to Cana."

His mind was elsewhere, but he agreed. The next
    day, Mary, Jesus, and the disciples
    set off for Cana.

A wedding, that most public gathering of friends,
    family, strangers, and they
    had a crisis.

The embarrassed family told her wine was running
    out. She did not say:
    "Why tell me?"

Instead, she told Jesus. Her smile contradicted his
    rebuttal: My time is not yet.
    "Do as he says."

Late into the wedding festivities, fresh wine
    flowing, Jesus asked her,
    Now I begin?

Smiling outwardly, inwardly riven, she softly,
    sadly, touched his face, replied,
    "Son, you have begun."

Questions for Reflection

At the Gate

1. Recall a time when a person whose arrival you eagerly anticipated did not arrive. How did you feel? Do you think that this is what Mary often felt in the short years of Jesus' ministry?
2. Scripture tells us little about Joseph. Do you imagine that Mary was a young widow by the time Jesus entered his late teens or early twenties?
3. If so, do you see Mary as the major figure in the formation of the Jesus of the Gospels?
4. Here we see Mary on a journey of faith, of not knowing exactly what was in store but pondering and trusting in God. How do you relate to this picture of Mary, as compared with the notion, implied in popular piety, that Mary serenely and knowingly complied with a prearranged divine script?

The First Journey: The Port

1. Describe the emotions you feel when you are leaving, or when someone is leaving you. Sorrow? Fear? Gratitude for the moments you had?
2. Is Jesus being selfish when he leaves his mother and work to travel and learn?

3. Can you see where many of the stories in Jesus' parables could have come from his real-life experiences? Identify a few suggested by this section.

To Caesarea Maritima—and Beyond

1. The Gospels indicate that Jesus was a normal boy subject to obeying his parents. At the wedding at Cana, Mary takes the initiative to suggest that Jesus can do something to help the newly married couple who have run out of wine. As you see it, does this in any way conflict with Jesus' identity as Son of God?
2. The story of Jesus and young Stephen is rich with biblical allusions. Can you name a few?
3. Do you know any women who are "wise without schools"—that is, women who never had much education and yet possess a natural learning along with their wisdom?

Purifying the Waters

1. The story of Jesus and young Stephen continues. Can you find additional biblical allusions in it? Could Jesus have learned how to deal with his disciples through his experience with this apprentice? Do you think Stephen is based on a real person in Scripture?
2. Already the youthful Jesus anticipates that one day he will have to challenge the religious establishment. Would Mary have been comfortable with that?
3. Do you think that Mary had any sense that the path her son felt called to take would ultimately lead to his death? How must she have felt about that?

The Road Back from Samaal

1. What must it have been like for Mary to have a son who appeared to the outside world to be a drifter—someone who liked to wander instead of following the accepted custom of setting himself up in his father's trade?
2. What role do you think an intense prayer life would have played in Jesus' developing awareness of himself and his mission?
3. Do you know any mothers who have made a great effort to further their children's sense of mission or self-fulfillment, even when the mother has not been totally comfortable with the chosen path?

Ezekiel's Grove Benediction

1. Some of Jesus and Mary's most important encounters take place in Ezekiel's Grove, a place named for one of the major Hebrew prophets. Do you see any significance in this? Who is the prophet here: Mary or Jesus? Or both?
2. Do you think Mary would have experienced the effects of Jesus' run-ins with the religious authorities, perhaps through neighbors' disapproval or scarcely concealed local gossip? How must that have felt?
3. Do you prefer to think of Mary as human and approachable—say, a hard-working wife and mother—rather than as the sweet, docile woman in the sometimes overly pious and saccharine depictions of her? Or is depicting her humanity a disservice to her?